Dove Over Clouds

Dove Over Clouds

Yolanda Nieves

Plain View Press
P. O. 42255
Austin, TX 78704

plainviewpress.net
sb@plainviewpress.net
1-512-441-2452

Copyright Yolanda Nieves, 2007. All rights reserved.
ISBN: 978-1-891386-67-1
Library of Congress Number: 2006938469

Cover art: *Palomas* © Sandra Posadas, 2006.

Acknowledgements

Grateful acknowledgement is made to the editors of the following presses in which some of these poems first appeared:

"A Mother's Wish" and "Real Men Make Tamales" appeared in *Heal: Between the Pages of These Folks We Seek a Panacea*, edited by Gladys E. Peres-Basheir, 2004.

"I Dreamed" and "Shame" appeared in *The Bilingual Review*, Arizona State University, 2004.

"Thrift Shop" appeared in *The North Central Review*, 2004.

"Puerto Rican Migration" appeared in *Dialogo Center for Latino Studies Magazine*, 2005.

Contents

I. Migration – Dove Over Clouds   7

Dove Over Clouds   9
Daydream 10
Kitchen   11
I Dreamed   12
All I Had Was Rita Moreno   13
Piano Music   15
A Mother Thinks About Her Daughter
   Who Crossed the Border   16
Remembering Julia   17
A Reason To Be Confused   18
That's Her Life   19
A Mother's Wish 20
From a Documented Emigrant To An
   Undocumented Immigrant   21
From Fire 23
Thrift Shop   24
What She Knows 27
At Fourteen   28
Teased To Death In a Housing Project   29
Shame   31
Butter   32
Sister   33
The Letter   34
Woman Alive   35
Puerto Rican Migration 1950   36

II. Isolation–The Whiteness of Silence 39

The Whiteness Of Silence   41
Advice To a Good Daughter   42
First Trip To Puerto Rico 43
Perhaps   45
Last Summer In Our Backyard   46
Distance Between Leaves and Dreams   47
What Do I Do With My Life Now?   48
No Regrets   49

How Will They Remember Us? 50
A Teacher Struggles With a Student On
    Deeply Personal Terms   51
Blame   53
A Child In the City   54
Woman Inmate   55
You Waited Until the End   57
Confession At a Grave Site   60

III. Liberation – For the Woman Who Asked For a Guacamole Recipe **63**

For the Woman Who Asked For a Guacamole Recipe 65
Isolation 67
Parking Lot 68
Sha'ir For the Girl In My Dream Who
    Stands By a Wall in Palestine 69
Advice To a Friend Who Has Considered Suicide 71
A Puerto Rican Girl Has a French Wet Dream 72
Zydeco Bar 74
A Whole Landscape Mine To Keep 76
Waiting 77
Sorry Times 78
Leaving You On 42nd Street 79
The World's A Mess After a Divorce 81
I Meant To Tell You 83
Runaway Lover 84
Like Me 85
Real Men Make Tamales 87
Dearest Family In Puerto Rico 88
This Place of Desire 90
Hoping You Return 91
Your Eyes In Mine 92
Nothing But a Dove Over Clouds 93

About the Author 95

1. Migration –
Dove Over Clouds

Dove Over Clouds

When I was a child
I lived as a dove

flying invisible against the cups of wind
over the swell of black noise

I agree only to light on a branch
where a chrysalis sways

hovering between the question mark of a riddle
that waited for the answer of my hymn

there I puffed my breast
full of a quiet flowing

flapped out the ache of sadness with my eyes
prayed myself into a morning

at times the profane pelted me
I made a new story shaped like a pearl

I never wanted a
shell for a heart.

Daydream

You could be looking out a window
floating in a daydream
in a second you are a falling star
air on water
this time flying over your childhood

visible for a moment
in the plaza of your eye
you grasp how sad your mother was
carrying the weight of complaints
without speaking.

You notice the graceful moon curves of her body
how her back bends humbly into work
mop in hand, hard breaths,
beads of sweat tracing her temple;
she stands to rub her bulging belly

music trilling on the radio
the kind she used to dance to
children's laughter trickling
through the open window
third floor rear.

For a moment a smile traces
the landscape of her face
something changes forever
it fills you strangely
you stand facing her gaze

a reflection travels far beyond her
to settle in your eyes.

Kitchen

I want to sit
at my mother's
kitchen table

a woman's world
where their laughter
ripe with sun

spreads like the orange of a yolk
their voices titter like rain on a tin roof
news from home

bread sprinkled sweet
I am weaved cheerful
against the winter outside

tonight the young girls
apprentice the art
of balancing salt in a spoon

the heart of each grain
of rice spoken for
crackling over fire

gossip is skinned and boned
the men invisible
smoking in another room.

I Dreamed

I dreamed
of being an earthly
plump
Spanish olive
desiring to be seduced
by the freshly grated garlic
that swims in the oil
conspiring with the vinegar
to bathe me nude
then impregnate me
with soft red peppers
only to be enclosed
in a crystal bottle
to be kept
not to be bruised
on the trip to
a salivating mouth
to be deliciously
devoured.

All I Had Was Rita Moreno

The Spanish neighborhood theater
in the Puerto Rican side of town
spangled lights, neon silver and gold

inside I sit mute
still as a porcelain figure behind glass
I pretend a new life, terrible and blessed
wait for light to enter my world.

She dances into the mouth of my heart
the splash of a comet
fierce passion
my honey and milk
crooned sweetness
grace of arms, legs, neck
slinging her hips wider than waves.

To be that
querida
you must own the universe
in a gallop of pride
I am languid in her light
the sweetness of the world may even return.

My happiness chews on the lips of the night
that my days are made up of mops and toilet lids
serious grief and doubt
is madness that shrinks rumpled under my feet.

continued

I am a sleeping girl roused
from the talons of invisibility.

I need not speak of anything else
it is enough to see her dance
she does not permit me to disappear
a lesson brandished like a spear
in my hand.

Piano Music

I haven't a clue of her
but the music is lovely
lures me like a prayer call
I pass by her apartment
stand and listen in the evenings
the music is lovely always.

If you stand here with me
you could listen
cry a little
I'll hold your hand
if you want me to
we can hear this
loveliness together.

Tonight this song is a wind
a flutter of wings, the wide open sea,
the breath of a sleeping child
not a skyscraper, or mountain, or temple.

Soon I'll walk on
when she looks up
she'll think no one stopped to listen
perhaps someone else will listen
to the silk of the keys
the sigh of the notes
its whispers and acclamations
and wonder who she is.

A Mother Thinks About Her Daughter
Who Crossed the Border

Her knees have spent years on the floor. They are callous from praying and scrubbing tiles in rich neighborhoods. The joints in her hands are bulbous from hard labor; they look beaded when locked in a prayer.

> *See the black and white photo of her daughter? The eyes are deep, a smile as wide as a country.*

Her daughter crossed *la frontera* to *el norte*. It is always north: Juarez, Loredo,Los Angeles, Seattle, Chicago, New York-the white frontiers. Clody. Cold. Most evenings she weaves fiber into tapestry, pulling under and over the loom bought with some money her daughter had sent

…some years ago.

A neighbor woman with a warm heart sits in a chair next to her. Quiet words tossed lightly back and forth across cloth and loom softens the chill that makes her throat tight as if a round stone had slowly grown there. She touches a letter in her pocket her daughter had mailed

…some years ago.

Some women quarrel and hold loneliness like a hot coal against their breasts. Others sit steamy biting their nails. Some women listen to music but do not dance. Others cry ceaselessly. This one sits by a window until morning holding the letter close to her breast, the ink in the letter faded.

Remembering Julia

> She died three thousand miles from Puerto Rico
> on a Puerto Rican Harlem street with no
> identification.
>
> Taken to a Potter's Field, she was buried in the
> standard pine box provided to paupers by city law.
> -Jack Aguero on Julia de Burgos, 1996

Unanchored, she wanted everything
to be the river
to find mercy in the wind
so pain
so permeable
would not torment
the lily of her heart.

Drinking the shape of words
I return to the place where
she weaved herself happiness,
                the river.

She was a floating dream, a soft stone,
a morning dove cooing since dawn
rolling through the waters of her life
holding close a lover,
                the river.

She drank the faces of the trees, the eyes of the moon
settled into a sad shadow of a cold city
wounded pressed into concrete
she slept that morning, and a lifetime away
still pulses her loneliness to us.

A Reason To Be Confused

My mother kneels on a cushion
tense against the pew.
as she prays a chain of memories
ring like tender little bells
a wild garden
a small farmhouse
her mother scooping up a chicken
with both hands.

I sit next to my father-his head digs deep
between his shoulders. He weeps into his hands.

Lilies and gardenias perch their petals near
the candles. A hand guides me to the casket.
My eyes pour over my grandmother's face.
I think how I tried to helped her catch
a chicken last summer, both of us laughing
as the cackling hens scattered in the yard.
To think of what I did not learn about her world.

They tell me she is sleeping. I can almost
see her breathe. I want to make her breathe.

That's Her Life

That's her life-
a barefoot run among tall grass
both green and dry;
a small figure leaning
against the cliffs of the years

at times she perches on a branch
where a leaf uncurls
a turquoise eye

her passion a small
bird in the rain
blown to the ground
in a valley winter white with silence

near the end
the finger of a lonely hour
points to the rustling of leaves
white muslin flapping
the clang of a bell heavy
in the distance.

A Mother's Wish

Your tender heart
a bleating lamb
soft batter arms
sticky like honey
swirl around my neck
when I hold you close
I can hear a tiny chirp
inside.
       Ven aca mi hijo.
Perch next to me
let us keep it
as it should be
you a freshwater pearl
hidden beneath its
tender pulp
a parchment kite
guided by a silver string
and tiny hands
a glowing paper lantern
hovering on a
purple summer night.
       Ven aca mi hijo.
A sleeping Titan
a mighty sword
a galloping stallion
you will awaken
too soon
too soon.

Your heart
my son
your heart
let me keep it
for you.

From a Documented Emigrant
To an Undocumented Immigrant

> Emigrate-to leave a country or region to
> settle in another.
> Immigrate-to come into a new country,
> especially to settle there.
> *Webster's New World Dictionary*

I know you must cross desserts and mountains, even an ocean. The nights are frigid and tight like a fist. You will walk under the heat of the sun. Hope grows like wild onions you are forced to eat. You carry a knife but it cannot cut the web of melancholy that has spun around your dreams. To pay for emergencies your uncle sent you money curled in a rubber band, stuffed in a sock. A woman walked between blue and black, this money tucked under her breast. She knocks at your door. Her story is another story. You are to tell no one you have any.

Your father shook your hand and sniffed into his dusty handkerchief. Your mother boiled eggs, wrapped some bread and cheese in a cloth, tucked it into your hands. She held you so tight your breath shrank in your eyes while she wept in her apron-the one you gave her last year. That night your neighbors lit a candle, held their rosaries a bit tighter praying *vaya con Dios*. Reaching the bend in the road you glance back one last time. Your eyes stretched to engrave the horizon in your heart. It throbbed in your throat.

Stuffed into a freight truck or a cargo ship, fifty others have the same dream. You wonder if there is room for all of you across the border. I did, too.

Our families arrive awkward together. We wash the same dishes, take care of each other's children, sleep to dream the same dreams, invent other lives. You are my brother. Your daughter is my daughter. Our hearts beg us to go home, our stomachs remind us of our hunger. We squeeze work like a woman does water from her

continued

hair. In this country we are whispers, an echo bleeding only after our day's work. Eyes erase us. We tiptoe not to startle the hope that flutters tiny. We will not be ashamed of our fifteen syllable name. I want to pour the strength of stones into your eyes and make our exile weightless. We can't reach where we want to go alone.

This poem can be translated into any language.

From Fire

From fire comes a woman's dream
forged from her life of bruised days

fatigue souring her bones
day after day spent standing

in an assembly line of parts
the red-raw hands, curved back

standing strong for her daughter's sweet nectar smile
she hides the weight of work swirling in her throat

what hurts her inside makes
an orchard of trees

a red jubilance of love
impossible dreams will fill out flesh

her daughter's life will hold a basket of ripe fruit
shades of sun will fill a field of flowers.

Thrift Shop

The air is rancid as if a woman forgot
to take a bath
and scrub her underarms
a reminder that the hanging blouses
shined over leather shoes
jeans and pajamas
frying pans and dusty books
once belonged to someone else

these are bargains for the poor
my mother and I roam the aisles
we agree on silence
looking for the orange ticketed items
they are half off today
tomorrow it will be the green
these are the prices for those
who inherited poverty

strolling our shopping cart
we scrutinize the racks
pretending we are women of leisure
this afternoon
cautiously eyeing others
preferring not to be identified by
a neighbor; knowing when to turn
our faces just so

I am in the book section
coveting the heroines painted
on the dusty romance novels
with breasts spilling over the
top of their dresses
I don't wear a bra yet
my mother admires a silk blouse

the color of a gray evening
buttons missing
a small rip in the sleeve
two crystal wine glasses
one engraved *bride*
the other *groom*
gleam in our cart
where my mother has placed
an oil painting of a tree
with branches the shape
of women's legs
the frame slightly bruise
a pair of overalls
pocket fastened with a pin
she will give it a new face
a yellow dress with
a tiny tear in the can-can
a secret I will keep
and wear it on Sunday
after she washes it twice
tonight

black scarf folded soft like
a woman's hair
in her hands
my mother's head slightly shakes as
her fingers graze
the bottom of her purse
to count the silver and
copper coins
the naughty ones clinging to
the bottom

continued

I imagine the riches
of the woman who
discards her designer dress
after wearing it only once;
it must be beautiful to
live how she lives
drinking champagne
in the afternoon
toes wading in a pool
white teeth shining
in the sun
her pink-cheeked children
staining the snow with
hot chocolate in Switzerland
while my mother cleans
her house.

What She Knows

My mother's voice echoes from the third floor window
the early evening punctured, interrupting the flock of children;

It's time to come inside
evil boys will spin rumors
about girls who stay out late.

What does my mother know of the evil in this world?
She was raised by an old sweet river made complete
by the fish she could touch with her fingers
coffee beans flavored her youth
feet free of shoes
a scar on her leg the only road connecting her
to the town she once loved
its memory makes her heavy.

Sometimes I wonder who she is;
I've barely met her.

I skip over the cracks in the cement to her voice;
she's setting out the anchor of dinner
pearls of sweat suspended against her temple
her belly round, ankles swollen
veins like crackling rivulets run through her legs
the scar yawning round like an eye.

Later she will press a cool towel against her forehead,
her lids quivering, eyes rolled up tight into little balls.

At Fourteen

A young girl begins to dream while she stares at the sun setting in the window. She believes that fire has taken over her. There is no rescue from the clanging in her ears. It is a sin to think of love in such a furious way. Everything else in her sits idle. She dreams of a heroic boy, becomes two breasts that need to be nibbled. The feminine mist of her petals burst. Her joy changes to shame as her skirt is pulled up above her head and they come in from all directions to her private zone shoving it in and out, white and thick-ugly She floats and thinks how empty she feels. Her mind becomes blank like a sheet of darkened ice. She closes her eyes, holds them tight. Echoes. Only echoes. The window is a dull flame. She doesn't know their names but will remember their stench on her forever. She has disappeared completely.

Teased To Death In a Housing Project

For a dead girl of twelve
her hair could not be more beautiful

her lips and nostrils seem to quiver
but her cheeks are flat, her brows too serious.

She used to laugh easily.

It is a hard place to be-in a pine box
soft mumbling, heads shaking

>> *what a shame*
>> *such a shame.*

Some hands try to touch her
some lips try to whisper in her ear.

Soon a flower will be planted over her heart.
It happened so fast. In that moment

it seemed that death was laughing at her
the sidewalk rose to swallow her

hands that pushed her over
the railing shrank away

children used to make fun of her
as if she tasted bad

they would never be sorry the way
she wanted them to.

continued

An angry mother cursed them
waved her fist

while they jumped the fence
throwing words like stones

breaking a mirror.

Shame

My mother has created a solitary alliance
miserable in the dampness of the morning
of her own design; she is like the wind
stripping shelves of beer bottles and gin
baptizing rugs in water and bleach
while my father's mouth opens to the ground
he hangs over the porch banister.

No speck of dust flicker today
in the personal corners of her room
cold walls clean house
my father brings an emptiness
that refuses to be swept away
an ember of despair flies
in her eyes

as she finds an empty
pint of Puerto Rican rum
like a broken bell
under the bed
it invades her privacy
the white of her space
draped on her shoulder

a cloak of winter
not worn proudly
it protects her from the
shame of their own design
of the years,
the many
years.

Butter

Hot wind bursts
through an open door
    third floor rear.

Uncovered butter
melts on the table.

Lucha Villa's crying voice
keeps us company.
    The radio trembles on the refrigerator.

Pork lard splatters
on the stove.
My mother's back side
sways
sings along.
I watch.
She doesn't notice me.
    My hand surrenders.

Squeezes the butter
my finger a spoon.
Scoops it up
dissolves in my mouth
like ice cream.

Sister

Esa mujer es picosa
grew chili pepper tangy
in a bellowing woman's womb
did handstands and backbends
spilled into the foam of life
like volcano and lava
her howl cayenne pepper red.
Ay, *mama* what happened?
What happened with her?

It's her way or no way
that hurricane of destruction
daggered tongue
smoking gun woman —
I say there is too much
bubbling Arawak blood of war
flowing through her veins.

That blade in her boot and
machete in her eyes
heart of a scorpion
fang of a snake
that descendent of fire
a menace to our tranquility.

Something steamy rises
when she walks into a room
she says things
and takes things
a woman on the prowl
I know her
how I know her.
Ay, *mama* what happened?
What happened with her?

The Letter

I kneel on the sofa listening
to what's important

my sister reads poems and
a letter she's found in a box

our mother's
never mailed-

she was married during the epiphany
flew to Chicago

the first night was cold-
almost lonely

she shrugged into her new life
refusing to be glassed in

somehow she became tree
her toes digging into the roots

of silence.

Woman Alive

I raise my glass
to the pure water of love
perpetual root of existence
fire
that's all I own-

fire.

I am blood
gathered in a flawed body
blended with the gravel of living
my eyes are two worlds
joined in an axis of fate

Is there a choice but
extend my arms
catch the sun
walk in the explosion
of each moment?

I live
sometimes without voice
sometimes without body
never without fire.

Puerto Rican Migration 1950

Years ago there was a way of living,
a rough manner on an island
the cane burst through the red mud
the sweat on the brow
of a tired cane-cutter man was all he
could drink. His son will have better.

There was a boy who swung
a machete against the cane
for so long his arms
grew as thick as a mango tree.
he raised his machete
waved it frantically,
        Estoy aquí. Trabajo con dolór.
        Hay tanto dolór que no hay donde esconderlo.

A plane flew carrying the boy
with a strong spine, ripe muscles
hopes like flames burning through fear.
the boy flew so far away
his pain became a tiny thing inside of him.

In this new country he became
a follower of his own shadow
a tongue stuck to the back of a throat
a reflection stretched gray on hotel dishes
hollow like his hope
eyes red from the fire of work
he lost the memory of why he had come.

The young boy became an old man
the old scars could not cover the older ones

he remembered his father carrying
the cane, a sweet sister, laughing boys.

Holding grief his feet stomped the pavement
raising his eyes he cried frantically,
      Estoy aquí. Trabajo con dolór.
      Hay tanto dolór que no hay donde escondérlo.

He did not want to forget how it was
hope became a tiny thing inside him.

11. Isolation—

The Whiteness Of Silence

The Whiteness Of Silence

My childhood? I lived it under the paws
of a phantom afternoon
an uninhabitable corner
where I curled inward
watching;

as my father tied the dog up with a chain
and left it in a darkened basement
until my mother tried to feed it
and it bit her
tearing at her flesh
until she became still.

From then on the roaches
outnumbered our plates
the birds decayed on the sidewalk
no one would sweep them up.

I turned into a cold stone
anchored by the unforgiving
whiteness of silence
living in a spell
where I waited to gather
strength to find my eyes.

Laughter, if possible,
will come later.

Advice To a Good Daughter

I give you permission to be *sin verguenza*.
to walk in a world of smokey cigars, carburetor oil
and broken beer bottles without shame.

Don't eat your inside out waiting for
the dance to begin
or speak only when you are spoken to
or sit on a chair like a package strapped
by ribbons and bows.

Wear your tattoo proudly. Let your eyes meet
theirs head on. Bellow out the truth. Let your
words sting like sunburn. A dart hitting a bull's eye.

Step in some mud. Rub it in someone's face
once in awhile. Run into the rain without
an umbrella. Drink tequila straight from
the bottle. Sing your songs hardy and late
into the night until you laugh and cry
at the same time.

Come home late without a proper excuse
embroider your own life
then sleep in a prayer.
Yes, *mi hijá*,
I give you permission to be
sin verguenza.

First Trip To Puerto Rico

Once, walking on a dirt road in Puerto Rico
sun streaming an impossible heat
I stopped by a river

sat to cry by the edge of it
flowering morning glories
escaped my tremors

this place is a dagger plunging
into the pulp of a tragic past
I want to be embraced with belonging

the way my mother was born into pineapple nettles
the way my father's breath was nailed to the stalks of cane

devilish history of hunger
womb of wanting
in me a lineage of blood

crashed into the deep concrete of a city
my cup trembles with years of space
between here and there

this scar of remembering
adhesion that will not heal
away from you I am a shred of afterbirth

the thread of a fish net ties me between
this world of sudden wind
chamber of sweet and bitter

continued

island of sea foam, sleeping gods
the red mud of me
silver gem on my forehead

revolving always in your orb.
I want to be embraced with belonging.

Perhaps

in time
a bird will light on your window
ignoring the slats of dusty blinds
to gift a song
forgetting you are surrounded
by vacant lots
all your reasons, whittled by knives
dissolve into the trash cans below
no longer a silent child of stone

perhaps-

your father who traveled too far into his pain
a windowless place
inflamed by something violent
his heart a throbbing cold fist
is suddenly still
becomes a web a roots
stiff between an orange morning
and a violet night
where he is the one afraid to close his eyes

perhaps-

in the space between branches and leaves
where neither shade or light reflect
you walk toward what you have left,
your heart the silver needle of a compass
points where you want to be;
a rose ripening under the green crest of the moon
where your quiet lies safely.

Last Summer In Our Backyard

The sun dives into the kitchen
a morning flame in your hair

outside you hose your feet, the neighbor's
dog, the tomato plants

their plump fists will be heaped in a bowl later;
a season winks with the moist birth

of shameless eggplants, green peppers, your favorite
music on the radio, our chatter, sweaty glasses of pink lemonade

in the center of the day we are divided
into work and play

sunset lets our toes languish on grass
until the purple of the horizon withdraws backward

counting fireflies soon tires us; bodiless sky
ripe with stars, the deep goblet of our eyes

flush with sleep, the depth of the day
sweet with color of sleeping leaves.

Distance Between Leaves and Dreams

I sit under a shadow of longing
the years a wheel that spins until it leaves me
daughter-orphaned; under the wavering branches
of the oak tree we saw grow and climbed in the backyard.

In my memory, the distance between the leaves and
the ground was small enough that if I held you
high enough your fingers could grasp the leaves.

One night, not extraordinary in any way,
except you were swollen with anger
harsh words hurled burning me;
clothes in a plastic bag slung over your shoulder
you left
a path
of time
has widened by words left unspoken

no pause to ease your fury you held it tight to your chest
your anger has shattered the stone of my resilience
forgetting the well of my love, or how my heart rose
like the waves of the sea when I watched you breathe.

I am stretched tight in this longing
this longing that lingers

in the blurred dull morning
under a shadow
branches waving
only the distance left behind.

What Do I Do With My Life Now?

I sit alone in an empty house. No one calls and asks mom what's for dinner? I no longer reply red beans and rice. We always have the same thing my daughter would say, and I'd reply there are starving children in the world that would be happy to take your place. I no longer ask her, can you go to the store, when I need a can of tomato sauce. Or have her look at me and ask can I keep the change? Yeah, you can, but don't talk to strangers, come right back. I no longer hear, you know I won't. It turns out I can't send her to the store anymore or ask you how's school? Or have her sit next to me to watch our favorite show because I'm too damn mad at myself for having given her everything, and she rebelled, and ran away from home, found her own apartment, and won't even speak to her father when he comes to knock at her door to see how she is. I heard her wish us death. She yelled it loud just before she left.

No Regrets

I don't regret where I'm going
I do not want to recall your eyes
like hazy clouds
squeezed tight
in both hands

with the weight of
a thousand raindrops
on your shoulders;
we all brush against time
vanishing like sleepy hours.

I will change granite into flowers
released into the color I really am
pass into the inside circle of endlessness
where the mouth of the sun opens
to swallow me.

I see my reflection next to yours
made of light
in time your footing will be steady
that's all I ask of you,
don't cry.

How Will They Remember Us?

I sit clutching your hand.
The quickness of years has left us open-mouthed
we are witnesses to the carting of children
into the fire of the wars
shaking our heads we let our voices smolder
like old letters in a trash can.
Perhaps the wars are too big to notice?
Our preoccupations have made us unconscious-
don't we regret it now?

Our arms waved the children away-our tongues
even cursed them at times; a boy with a dream
in his hands insisted on following us asking
who am I? We looked away.

We made them stop to pay attention;
erased the imaginings of stories, of the
pictures they painted. Swept from the
playgrounds by sour bells we tucked them
tight in a room, made them stare
eyes straight ahead. What was wrong with
letting them tug on a petal, swing from a tree,
or keep a wild sparrow in a shoebox?

What have we become? A hardened place where
a tender spot should be? No one of them will come back
for us if their arms cannot become wings.

A Teacher Struggles With a Student
On Deeply Personal Terms

You strut in with gang signs in your eyes
I arrive with books under my arms
you have lived on the streets where
the cry of your mother has become broken glass
your father's belt buckle a scar on the edge of your eye
his fist a split bone in your nose.

We sit in a room
until we find a story we can share
a short one for a short time
it keeps you from gazing out the window
from becoming a cloud.

My hope for you hangs on the edge of a cliff
all day I hope – giving you new things to consider
I study your eyes – they are black birds
detached on a branch
detached from my words
across the street young boys
rise up and explode.

What is a book to us if we cannot read
our own stories or utter our own names?

I cannot make you copy the problems
on the board; you have too many of your own
what happened last night –
the body shot down next to you,
cops pulling back your neck
thrusting their clubs into your ribs
until you screamed
these are the subjects that worry you
a book will not help now.

continued

I do not know how this story flew away
and became a small thing over us
I want to remember your eyes;
they have wings.
I keep your desk by the window
a pencil and paper ready for you.

Blame

Chicago, home of the political machine
June 25, 1970
my father sits on a stool at the local bar
to write a brief note:
"Dear Rose," he starts to pencil on a napkin
but the jukebox plays his favorite song
one of the few he remembers from Vietnam
his buddy from the sanitation department
who drives the garbage truck jaunts in,
sleeves rolled up to his armpits
slaps my father on the back
tells him not to worry.

They have some drinks–no one is counting
he relives the moment when the
boss's secretary and mistress suspects
the cash box break-in is his doing
even though he wasn't there
the key was found in his locker
that's what he will tell my mother.

Hours later driving his Chevy
east on North Avenue the
sky heavy and humid
he hammers the accelerator to the floor board
car hopping over the curb
into the dead fish in the water
the wind helps carry the car beyond the bridge
he can't remember I'm tucked in the back seat sleeping
while he lets his breath take in the sting of the water.

Since then I've been distracted, my will usurped
by the coldness of water-his weapon
me floating like a discarded apricot pit
on an old Chevy tire.

A Child In the City

A child in the city
had a name
he was found with a borrowed book
under his arm
a note in his pocket from
his teacher saying,
...*did very well today*
next to the bullet hole
in his chest.

Tomorrow
his mother will cry over his face
her thumb tracing his eyebrows
a little brother limp by her side
an old man will weep in his handkerchief

a politician will vote for more jails
while police sit smoking cigarettes
in their cars

they think that guns slung on
their hips is better than
a boy with a book.

In some parts of the city
only the littlest children
can send laughter into the air
while the houselights are dimmed
blamed is uttered quietly and
more blisters of smoke are
are heard on the street.

Woman Inmate

She is the vapor
of an afterthought
her body a ripe violet plum
flung to the ground
pulp exposed

this time her husband
in one last struggle
bleeds dead
a kitchen knife
the last wave of their lives

her back leans
limp against a concrete wall
cruelty has cemented
her tongue
so little air to breathe

in her dreams her hand
caresses the face of her son
he sends her a poem
written on a paper bag

when her eyes wander
out of her head
she falls into a blackened hole-

she crushes a cigarette
beneath the heel
of her shoe
the socket of her heart
burns empty

continued

from the courtyard
through the clouds
she sees her name
dangling from a branch

of a dying tree.

You Waited Until the End

(for Eric)

My father drunk
he wore the face
of being beyond
the reaches of thought

my mother scrubbed toilets
then walls
for her
always the same day
the same night

your mother silent
afraid
the purple iris
of a budding bruise
near her cheek
the final say
of a conversation
with your father

later the pentecostal
church bus
takes them away

what they were doing
had splinters
a hollow center
they barely knew us
barely brushed up
against us
always a nervous
step backward

continued

we filled our days
with our own recipe
what we did had sweetness
asking for nothing
watching some birds fall
other fly
time blur

we knew we were
innocent
from the way
our eyes held
the day
walked through them
as if they had
nothing to do
with us

we told each other
we were born
for something else
to have stars
and oceans
laugh in our hearts

in the silence of time I lost you

you entered
the threshold of illness
hospital rooms
bulging sores
skin sticking to bones
people you never knew
wiping your body

not much more
news than that

Did you think
I forgot you?

There are nights
I shake my fist
at the moon
the liquid spread
of tar
in my veins

the endless surprise
of missing you
fills me up

when I am sleepless
the cold fire of
my eyes
burns at the sky
my hands are
grey ashes
covering my heart
I know you
expected me

all the time

you waited
until the end.

Confession At a Grave Site

I must speak to the dead
while there is still light;
each word a flutter of black wings-
keeping my promise
is like a hammer
trying to shatter the sea.

I cannot claim that the morning birthed me,
my first breath was a groan,

>*you knew this.*

Why trust me when failure has been ironed on my chest?

Time has squeezed me
into a tiny gasp;
I have landed in a place
where I cannot tell
when the black of the sky melts into the
gray of the morning.

This promise is a blind inner eye
a stuttering tongue
a broken foot crawling
away from the heels of light
I cannot keep
this promise
>*this promise*

has hung off a cliff for too long
it wants to sleep;
I need to walk away to
what I have left
a direction that gathers
in the folds of my belly
dense as a fog
unfettered to you.

III. Liberation – For the Woman Who Asked For a Guacamole Recipe

For the Woman Who Asked For a Guacamole Recipe

First:
turn your face to the sun, breath in the dawn
the damp air, the earth, and roots
mutter a prayer in a language you heard only once before
walk barefoot in a vaporized field
let your feet grip the earth-let them become
like the arteries of a fertile womb
until you find the avocado tree that you have known
since its infancy.

Second:
the tree you know grows short on purpose-
a welcoming sign
the avocados, like the eyes of a dolphin, glow green
they wave;
from this canopy of branches name one,
let it become as clear as your own face
it will drop into your hands.

Third:
in the chamber of a bowl the pulp bobs up
effortlessly like a body in an ocean
and will shed its skin from its own accord
this will be as intimate as honey on the lips
stir in the tartness of a lemon,
the piercing sting of a little onion
only if you honor cilantro and garlic
sprinkle it in.

continued

Last:
This is the difficult place-an equation of hope
go back to your prayer
there must be a motion of faith
hum quietly as you swallow
there it is-
if it is not enough
stand still and become a small breathing thing
under the avocado tree.

Isolation

Women cannot ignore
the symptoms
piped running water
brings us

we live in a dangerous silence
no village of women
surround us

we cannot even sit
silently together
to be relieved of the need
to be angry

Nigerian women are lucky
they have to walk to a well
for water

they know each other
they sip the tears that fall
from each other's cups
understanding

no one of them is expendable
as the morning sky opens
together they swallow the world

embrace each other
and wonder
how do we speak to each other
here?

Parking Lot

They stood there for a hundred years
a theater of trees

in patches of order
branches like fingers touching

bark ponderous and proud
leaves a flock of sparrows chirping

boisterous in the air
the wine and bread of a garden's belly

the whirr of a sudden uproar
a stiff crackle, a bursting fall

broken towers, pulp sliced into nudity
a swarm of flies is released

circus of steel blades erases a backyard forest
the circle count of years a tombstone

their absence touches my forehead
a puncture in the sky

in the eye of my heart.

Sha'ir For the Girl in My Dream
Who Stands By a Wall In Palestine

Stopping to read the slogan on the crumbled wall
she is sure a prophet stood there once
and remembers this road used to have a name.
Surrounded by women, they are
the keepers of tears, the breakers of stones
the pail of water becomes lighter in her hands.

Aware of the barbed wire curling behind her
she fears the teeth that wait to bite the flesh
of any boy who wants to cross.
In this place dust swirls all the time
so do prayers.
Everyday there are funerals
no one asks *What happened here?*

The stump where her uncle's olive tree
use to grow sits stubbornly
roots still grasping the heart of the earth
declaring the one thing that really matters
I am not a refugee! I am a citizen!

When the bulldozers came she thought
that if she waited until morning
everything would be over
but the violence is a shadow always looming
from the west like a wicked weed
curling over and around
choking every hope that dares to grow.

continued

In her pocket her fingers rub an olive
seed as large as the moon.
She has decided to plant it one day.
It will be a quiet morning
the dust will have settled
the tree will grow like a poem
doves will settle on the branches
she will name the tree
yemken boukra because
for every death, there is a birth.

Advice To a Friend Who Has Considered Suicide

Consider planting rose bushes
in your back yard
and one big tree.
In the winter
watch them pause
under the snow.
In the summer spy on
them where the grass
can caress our feet.
Hold your eyes steady
in the blue of the sky.

When it rains,
especially when it rains,
hold your own hand
don't let go.
Listen to the moaning
all around you.
Gather any seeds
scattered by the wind
count them
plant them deep into the earth
until the sun dries the mud
and a sunflower stands tall.

When it gets hot
sit under the tree
eat an apple slowly
pick a rose and
though the thorns
make you bleed
clutch it close to your heart
sing your name a hundred times
then call me if you need me.

A Puerto Rican Girl Has a French Wet Dream

go ahead
hold me captive
seal me in a porcelain jar
until the summer solstice arrives
then let me loose to dance
our pas de deux
a frenzy right into
the Seine River

indulge my passion
for Beaujolais
let the full moon come
and go
until it sinks into
the ocean
on the other side of
the continent

throw a satin sheet
on the garden dial
mark time with the
flutter of your eyelids
let's juggle our caresses
high into the air
your hands are planets
majestic
soaring like a jaguar
over soft terrain
deep and pink
you a Michelangelo sculpture
me a Venice canal
watery
warm

together we are frenzied
cyclists
you pedaling
me on the handle bars
jousting up and down
the Champs-Elysees
a thousand spectators
cheering our
stunts.

Zydeco Bar

The great alligator of music
from the distance beckons us
roll out from under the net of the night
the round tongue of the crescent moon
howls from the bayou
                   tonight
                   tonight.

The laughter of the water baptizes time
throw away your wristwatch
come alive
you know it's good for you
Zydeco dancing
here I go,
my black boots
in a cloud of accordions
I don't need a clue except
a bowl of gumbo
to yank the devil out of me.

Tonight we indulge
in affairs of the heart
our allegiance to the music
descending like rain
blazing like fire
while fleshly ladies puff on cigarettes
the red of their lips spreading in smiles
endless like the Mississippi
the cleavage of the music
enticing us all
                   drinking
                   winking

as the heat grows deeper
the night shorter
we are the heads and tails of the dance

as the pink hours of the dawn
arrive like a sparrow
the music whirls out the door
leaving us dizzy
its veneer still sweet on my mind
smooth as rain water dew.

it was good,
good for you, too.

A Whole Landscape Mine To Keep

The pink lips of the morning
not yet opened
your sleeping eyes
are like clapping castanets
your arms languish
on the sponge of my belly
while I inhale your breath
misty like the pampas
after rain.

I stretch my eyes
to your chest
mountainous
I don't know whether to
touch you with bare hands
or let you float
in the river of your sleep.

With my finger I trace
a lighthouse
an ocean
a ship
a dagger
I imagine a tree
I used to climb on

you a whole landscape
mine to keep.

Waiting

The clock behind the bar echoes midnight
next to me a man brags to his friend
how he left his woman at home. They laugh.
His black cigarette smoke burns acrid in my throat.

A couple on the dance floor floats mouth to mouth
swallowing kisses and tongues
I watch them take their pleasure
no one asks me to dance. I would refuse.

The room swells like cork in heat
my breath is squeezed in the palm of this waiting
I am the shape of an empty circle
in a tight grey place.
            Hurry.

While the hungry mouth of the night quivers
I bury the words that stand between you, me.
I wait the way I want to wait,

        listening to an endless wire of voices
        murmuring invented syllables

watching the slavery of their loneliness
eyes searching eyes
this is a place of ghosts
strutting,
grinning,
waiting.
            Hurry.

Sorry Times

Whether it's the glaze of him
or just the city's neon lights

whether he settles inside his shoulders
or erases himself in a darkened doorway

I cannot get used to the way I turn away;
my eyes avoid his loose-fitting flesh

scissoring deep to trim my path of him
I am a pocket stitched tight

he cannot become visible-not even for a moment
he is the tongue of sour wine

his belly an empty bread oven
the grill of hunger, bone of fear

as I walk by I feel the brush of cold night air
an execution is an axe falling only once

the flattened corners of a box under a bridge
shopping cart, newspaper, plastic carp a blanket

a mouth speaks to itself alone telling
stories of our sorry times.

Leaving You On 42nd Street

Buildings stand together
by the weight of contradiction
a landslide of concrete
every window is an eye

inhabited by shadow-less people
beaten black by the night
who descend into subway tunnels
inside the geometry of a city

your chose to evaporate
where subway lights flap like wings
among the bees nest
of sharp elbows and shoulders
you chose to evaporate
                      with them
                      like them.

where the slightest music
is washed away by
the growl of trains
punctual
linear.

I returned without you
to the ripple of the wind in an open space
under the sun's spreading lips
I have become green

continued

folded neatly among vines
that sprout tomatoes
the sadness in my throat
a mangled bird caught in a net;

on the forehead of aloneness
the sky is enormous
I will invent myself a new birth
become the roots of a tree

a brave cluster of clovers,
the quiver of a sigh.

The World's A Mess After a Divorce

so I stripped the bed
put out the cat
scrubbed the floor
wrote to my congresswoman
grilled vegetables
read my own tarot cards
stretched into yoga poses

dyed my hair
shaved my armpits
danced the electric slide
let in the cat
made a tail for a kite I intend to buy
held my breath while I
stared at my naked body
in the mirror

became afraid
then unafraid
identified a spot
for a pitchfork tattoo
smoked a cigar
burned a candle
drew a moustache on the
cover model of Cosmopolitan Magazine
then called to canceled my subscription

cursed my ex-husband
sharpened my kitchen knife
called my mother
sent ten dollars to
Save the Women foundation
crossed my fingers

continued

made a wish
found the Greenwich Meridian on the map

climbed on the fire escape
sat with the cat
stared at the moon
cried
listened to the cars grumble by
laughed and laughed
at the messiness of mess.

I Meant To Tell You

You have grown magnificent
like a red sequoia against the moon
like the space between the ocean and sky
where there is no end.

I have always loved you
I meant to tell you
but instead I dreamt of rain,
of a goldfish ready to become
an eagle in your eyes,
of your arms carrying me
from the city
to live outside of linear time.

All I could do was breathe your skin
so close to mine
like the heavy salt in the air
by the sea
like the hands of flames waving
between the wood in a hearth
you were preoccupied.

The light becomes water on your face;
I cannot go back to what I left,
we are together a little too late
these years between us
have spread our lives distant
like the leaves rioting against the wind
scattering to different directions

You magnificent against the moon
me a blade of grass beneath you.

Runaway Lover

This question is a circle
a small cry
with roots buried deep
in yesterday
I can't seem to find you
I am a woman gone dumb

dissolving in a black liquid
into the entrails of the ocean
my hand disjointed
fumbling to reach
the space where
there is a piece of you

my wound is pink
condemned to stay raw
I said one thing
you stayed away all night
the rooster of the morning
crows
where are you?

Like Me

> *But the poor are not fooled; they see*
> *the truth and speak out when*
> *others remain silent.*
> -A letter from a Christian group
> from Haiti to Gustavo Gutierrez, 1984

In the fields the sun presses its
tongue against her neck
bent over lettuce she cannot stop to talk
in the truck there is only room
for the bushels of potatoes
not for the pity or heaviness of my face
glancing at her from the highway.

Her eyes say *te conosco*, I know you.

Some say she is like all the field hands
come to plunder a rich country
the one who picks the grapes
the one who picks the apples
all the same.

I say she is like me.

In the city a woman will rinse
the lettuce and wonder
who ripped this heart from its root?

There is holiness in everything
in the scarred hands that hold the blade
in the feet crossing borders
in her eyes that say
si, we should talk a while

continued

our grandmother's love stories
the way our children laugh at the world
we might be able to hold hands
in the spaces between the fence.

Real Men Make Tamales

Who is this *charro*
that has lassoed my heart?
Quick stepping cowboy
ranchera spinning poet
with a '67 pick-up
parked on my lawn?
Spur whirling
pozolé-loving
tamale making man.
A singing rooster
in my kitchen.
He knows the ins and outs
of *masa* mixing
and *carne* filling.
He wraps those tamales tight.
Knocks the breath right out of them.
A real macho
Who is this woman that
let him in?
Rolling pin, tequila,
rodeo rope and all?
Who sits on the back
of his saddle?
Cowboy you have
lassoed all of me
out of my *fiesta* and
into your corral.

Dearest Family In Puerto Rico

The fury of Huracán
the Arawak love of dominance
the slave trade brand on the thigh of our history
the underground network of African saints
the fierce spice of Creole sin-
          stands like a thick white candle,
          the flame burns red
          alive inside
from far away
let's lessen the grief of distance
raise me like water to your lips to ease

the hunger of our cracked dry silence
the scalpel of forced sterilization
the pauper's grave of a cane cutter
the hundredth mountain charred for a highway
maracas that rattle fury
suitcase, rumpled handkerchief,
years of no return

I have cried like a stepchild
my single tear has a hundred more
together we walked into

the Chicago uprising 1966
a Young Lord's fist in our face
factory layoffs
the shameful shuffle for government cheese
a drafted son dead in foreign wars
our children's faces swell with not knowing

they ask for you
they cannot hold their vastness
our country is never one place
our veins run into one river

smooth me back into your palm
our distance has curled itself small in my eye
the future grows thick with the names of our children

dearest family in Puerto Rico-
the closed eye of our memory sleeps only a little.

This Place Of Desire

This place of fire and light
spreads like the purple of a bruise
it is a geography of flames
this desire
threatening the angles of my days
should I surrender
into an ocean
hopeless like a river that yawns
hopeless like silk that folds upon itself
like an dying woman
swimming into the sun on the horizon?

Witness
prisoner
victim
I am all of these
my blood hums
I cannot sleep
tumble into tunnels
        chasing the night with my eyes
        with thoughts of you

in that place
where we wake to
the yawning of stones
the first seeds of turquoise bud
the gold of the morning
blankets the blue of the night
my eyes become flowers
        your lips are birds carrying us beyond a cliff
        surrendering
to hopeless
desire.

Hoping You Return

Tonight my heart is filled with
mango meat and a shot of dark rum.
The sweet and bitter. This is the curse
of the living. We cannot be afraid.

Whisper my name and I am surrounded
by a flock of swans that rise in my throat
lie next to me and I am flushed by an ocean
rumbling its questions out loud.

Your hands seek all my secrets
I am conquered land
a white flag waving surrender
an outlaw woman running toward
the edge of a cliff.

We willingly cross borders
our flesh lighted candles
the cave of your mouth
swallows all of me
I am a tongue outstretched
like a net I gather all you give.

When you leave in the morning
I am a fist clenching itself raw.

Your Eyes In Mine

In my sky you are a cloud
color of silver, lining of blue.

Sing, I ask. You become a sparrow's throat.
Cry, I ask. You are a lamp that powders its light dim.

My day is a possession of wind and blood
a living haze of questions without you.

My life is a shell at the edge of the ocean
until your eyes wash into mine.

Our bodies cup into an evening blossom
the night's glance cannot mistake you

for a cold river.

Nothing But a Dove Over Clouds

Where was I last night?
What did I dream
but forget?

Pasó la noche
con lluvia en sus brazos
¿Como puede una paloma

seguir nada menos que el sol?
¿Donde iba?
¿Por las montañas?

¿A respirar el mar?
Mi papá andando en
la finca de caña

lucero prendido, descalzó,
sus ojos dos
tacitas de café

voz de cometa
en las nubes canta
¿Donde vas?

I can't remember
where I was last night.

Sigo a mi padre
en su sueño de olvido
murmullo de sombra

descansa
paloma
descansa.

About the Author

Yolanda Nieves, drawing from her Puerto Rican heritage, her experiences in Chicago's Humboldt Park neighborhood, and the impressions left on her by the women who directly and indirectly shaped her world view, gives us poems that reaffirm the strength of the human spirit. In her first full collection of poems, she captures the spirit of hope that belongs to all of us in a voice that is both soft and strong. Yolanda Nieves has a devoted following for her work as a poet, and has been published extensively by independent and university presses. Currently, she lives in Chicago with her family and teaches developmental reading at Wilbur Wright Community College.

www.ingramcontent.com/pod-product-compliance
Lightning Source LLC
Chambersburg PA
CBHW071023080526
44587CB00015B/2467